QUARANTINE

WITH YOU

Dedication

For Sharrod Jr. / S.J.

Printed in the United States of America
ISBN- 978-1-963964-16-5 (Print)
ISBN - 978-1-963964-17-2 (Digital)

Library of Congress Control Number: 2024927195

Published by Cocoon to Wings Publishing
7810 Gall Blvd. #311
Zephyrhills, FL 33541
www.CocoontoWingsBooks.com
(813) 906-WING (9464)

Illustrated by Lidya Riani

Message to Readers

This book is for all the families affected by the COVID-19 pandemic. During these trying times, many families prevailed and found the strength to carry on each day.

We've become teachers, multitaskers, Zoom-masters, full-time parents, nurses, and more. We've managed to DO all of this by keeping faith in GOD.

This pandemic has taken a lot from us all. It may not haveallowed us to be in the same space with each other, but somehow, it brought us closer together. We became creative, in many ways, with how we showed compassion and love for one another. From daily Facetime calls to celebrating birthdays and holidays, we managed to do all this with strong faith and knowing that everything would be alright.

God bless all of the families and loved ones affected by COVID-19. I CAN Do ALL Things Through Christ Who Strengthens Me. – Philippians 4:13

One day, life as we know
it changed overnight,
and it brought you closer to me.

I became your nurse,
teacher, and personal chef.

Teaching and learning with
you is so much fun.
"You are the best teacher!"
you would say proudly with a smile.

Lunchtime is your favorite part
of the day because you get to
sit right next to me.
"You make the yummiest lunch,"
you would say with a mouth full
of the cheesiest macaroni.

Our trips to the grocery store are much different now. I got us matching masks to make wearing them a little more fun.

I made your birthday extra special.
You did all the things you love to do,
like racing your fastest cars and trucks.
I was right there to cross
the finish line with you.

When we go on our walks, you draw pictures on the grey sidewalk. You draw pictures of spaceships with your colorful chalk. And I get a front-row seat to our art shows.

You come to work with me
every day. You file away your
ABCs as you pretend to work with me.

I look forward to movie night
with you. We eat the yummiest
snacks, and I get to
snuggle up right next to you.

I love the time I'm spending
with you. I like when we pretend
to be superheroes and when
we battle fire-breathing dragons.

Life has become a lot different;
much is unsure. But
it's okay because I get to
spend every day
with you.

About the Author

Jasmine Slatton is a certified phlebotomist who began her career at a leading hospital in Tampa, Florida. With over six years of experience in the banking industry and a background in customer service, she is passionate about connecting with and serving others. Jasmine is also a certified assistant coach for her son's little league baseball team and a devoted single mother who has faced life's challenges with resilience and faith.

During the COVID-19 pandemic, Jasmine found inspiration to write Quarantine with You, a children's book that celebrates finding hope and silver linings in uncertain times. Supported by her faith and a strong community, Jasmine has embraced her roles as an author, digital creator, and mother. Through her work, she shares her journey and creativity to inspire others, showing that even in difficult moments, there is strength and beauty to be found.